ENDANGERED SPECIES

ENDANGERED SPECIES

DAVID WALTNER-TOEWS

TURNSTONE PRESS

Published with the assistance of the Canada Council and the
Manitoba Arts Council.

Turnstone Press
607-100 Arthur Street
Winnipeg, Manitoba
R3B 1H3

This book was printed by Hignell Printing Limited for
Turnstone Press.

Printed in Canada.

Cover illustration: David Morrow

Cover design: Steven Rosenberg

Back cover photo: Kathy Waltner-Toews

Some of these poems have previously appeared in *Canadian
Author and Bookman*, *Contemporary Verse II*, *The Mennonite
Reporter*, *Journal of Mennonite Studies*, *Queens Quarterly*, and
in *Mennonite Blues*, a stage adaptation of the poems of David
Waltner-Toews, by Larry Danielson.

"The Gift" and Part I of "Images of Peace" were first
published in *Three Mennonite Poets* (Intercourse,
Pennsylvania: Good Books, 1986).

The series, "Images of Peace," was written for a conference
on "Peace and the Arts" at Conrad Grebel College,
University of Waterloo, in November of 1983.

Dates and places of composition follow the poems.

Canadian Cataloguing in Publication Data

Waltner-Toews, David, 1948-

  Endangered species

  Poems.
  ISBN 0-88801-126-1

I. Title.

PS8595.A485E5 1988   C811'.54   C88-098033-8
PR9199.3.W34E5 1988

this book is for Matthew and Rebecca

CONTENTS

I ALL HANDS ON DECK

November Light 3
A Basket of Years 5
Still Life, with a Mango 8
The Love Bite 10
Identifying a Tree in the Fall 12
Something Is Missing 13
Pastorale 14
What the Flying Woodchuck Thinks 15
Something I've Been Meaning to Tell You 17
All Hands on Deck 19
What to Pray For 21
Generations 22
Endangered Species 24
Silence: it is never the same 26
The Mind 27
The Heart's Dance 29
Poem for My Friends 31
New Directions in Growing 32
The Big One 33

II THAT OLD SCRAP AGAIN

There Might Not Be a Nuclear War 37
That Old Scrap Again 38
Conversion Experience 40
Images of Peace 42
Peaceful Linguistics 50
Alms for the Rich 51
For a Columbian Mother 52

III   SURVIVORS

The Gift 55

Mind out of Season 57

A Kind of Resurrection 59

Taking Heart 60

The Day Before Winter in Sutherland 61

Tante Tina's Christmas, 1983 63

Tante Tina Reflects on Maggie Thatcher 66

Tante Tina Calls in to a Radio Talk Show 68

Winnipeg 70

Iceland 72

Birds 73

Giorgio, Where Are You Now? 77

39 Lines for My 39th Birthday 79

The Poet's Ambition 81

Diver's Toast 83

At the Centre 84

What This Poetry Is All About 87

An Old Grey Water Buffalo in the Noonday Sun 88

TRANSLATIONS 90

I
ALL HANDS ON DECK

NOVEMBER LIGHT
for Jim and Ruth

Hesitant beside an opened cage door
we poise at birth
We cannot believe this is happening
this breathless ruffle
this life

The air tumbles with the scents of apples
pumpkins freshly dug carrots potatoes
black earth   trembles with the unsung carol
of cedar waxwings amid sprigs of red berries
and the white sigh of snow-breasts

In this brief infinity of hesitation
lurks the fear of being caught of not catching
blooms the flower
of forever-being-lost
the broken tongue's rough-stemmed bitterness

And as Fall sunlight
leafs between the trees' thorned crowns
we dance
like cats following birds in teasing leaps
we weave between the still trees circling
in the dance of tyrants' toppling
the dance of childhood
of almost catching almost being caught
catbird oneness   trailing bright threads
encasing ourselves this moment
in a cocoon of pure light

On January's muffled dark sea
I remember without thinking the bright turmoil
of that time   It is Eden
within me   left   and forever
returning   a gently cupped hand
a graceful ark of dreamtorn creatures
poised forever on a cresting wave

just above the ragged contours
of the inevitable reef

GUELPH, JANUARY 1985

A BASKET OF YEARS
for Kathy at her 36th birthday

When you get your first year
it's like a banana
Never having had a long yellow year
before   you're not sure
what to do with it
You squeeze it very hard
until it explodes   Delighted
you run mashed banana pulp
through your hair

By the second year
you're getting smart
You explode the year
then eat it

Soon you figure out
how to peel the time back slowly
nibbling away at the white cakey hours

Just when you think you've got
the hang of it
you get handed a pineapple
You try to peel it
as if it were a banana
Thirteen is a prickly sticky-handed year

It takes a few years
but you get handy with a knife
Things are getting sweet and juicy
You're learning to anticipate

When the apple arrives it's a surprise
but it's what you've been wanting
secretly   a smooth firm time
Nothing that can't be solved
with a bit of determination and a good
set of teeth   At first even
the tart times feel clean
on your tongue   but after a few years
you're picking out the sour ones
and mellowing them in pie
You have this time-passage thing
down to an art now

Then comes the big green football
Just about kills you
You chop away at it with a fruit knife
You work up a sweat over this one
Inside it's brown hairy and tough

This year's going to be a real coconut
you say   One after another
the years keep coming like passes
from a throw-happy quarterback

By the time you're thirty-six
you know how to give them
a good whack with a machete
You let the time gurgle down your throat
and dribble over your chin
In the shade of the palm tree
you spoon out the hours
one by one

not thinking about the shape
of years to come

JAVA, SEPTEMBER 1985

STILL LIFE, WITH A MANGO

The swelling rounded body
firm   giving slightly to the squeeze
stiff nipple where the stem was
reminds me of something

As it rests in my hand
fresh   as from a bath
I think of mountains in Java
a wet-nosed stallion muscular
but friendly nibbling from my palm
before he canters along the breathless
inter-paddy paths to a waterfall
Bright flowers hide like little children
aching to be found
among the green leaves

When the mango is opened
its flesh is firm and wet
inviting the intrusion of a tongue

It is the ocean on my body
after too much sun
the large wet hand of a wave
slipping down my limbs

The flesh of the mango is sweet and cool
filling the heat of a Javanese afternoon
with juice and happiness
The moment of its eating brims so full
there is no room for reflection

The stone of a mango
is love's secret
the heart's uncut diamond
slippery with memories

I hold it in my hand
I am satisfied

JAVA, SEPTEMBER 1985

THE LOVE BITE

The little brown bunnies
with their innocent tails
hop by on the spring-green grass
I love bunnies

The grey cat scampers after
so playfully after
where those innocent
bobkins have passed
I love that skitterish cat

Cat bites tails
Bunnies scream

Sadly   in my living
room   I stitch the innocent tails
back on to heart
broken bunnies

I take the warm little bodies
out to the woods
and leave them   knowing
they will die   Bambi and Thumper
none of whose best friends are feline
watch
They have small
manageable hearts   with no room
for cats

The cat has followed me
into the woods
I think he is behind
the poison ivy
The bunnies are thinking quietly
behind a rotten birch log

I am lost inside
the last wild place on earth
Little brown bunnies are hopping by
in the dusky darkening wood
Feels so natural
must be good

The poison ivy moves

GUELPH, SUMMER 1983

IDENTIFYING A TREE IN THE FALL

See how it is rooted
among shrubs and boulders
Often you will see it thus
salmon-coloured gnarled bark
bending upward quivering
into a red crown

Unlike for instance the red maple
this tree loves darkness
Unlike the bent jackpine
this seeks out warmth
Unlike even its own metaphor the mushroom
this flowers in a startling
burst of white blossoms

All at once the air is full
of honey bees
and the sweet stinging
of Nature

It is a short radiant season
withering unsapped
into the bee-less dark

Unlike say the buckthorn
if you touch these roots gently
there   between the boulders
you will feel the seedling stir
again   softly

GUELPH, OCTOBER 1984

SOMETHING IS MISSING
  (It Cannot Be Caught)

Our bodies are
the interslipping of a thousand fish
fins sensing almost touch
a thousand neural tips
in playful synchronicity   all rhyme
for no earthly reason

It calls for a poem
It begs for a net
When I oblige
what do I get? Haddock flopping
in a slippery pile
and   between the lines   into the deep
lost blue   a silver flutter

Friday the poet eats fish
sticks with ketchup   a good meal
but something short
of a religious experience

        GUELPH, FALL 1984

13

PASTORALE

When like a calf
you wobbled up through the brush
to suckle at the cherry-cheeked pear tree
I was lifted up into grace
floating just above the sunrise.
My head was a barn
from which I called
my voice distant
like a bird
a single dark wavelet
against the bright horizon.
And when you lay down your head
your hair sweeping as a willow
on the smooth of my belly
I became for you—
empty of all but you
your mouth
and the taste of your tongue—
a bed of straw.

GUELPH, MAY 1987

14

WHAT THE FLYING WOODCHUCK THINKS

Hawk wheels
high above the white cliffs
Woodchuck waddles out
from under rock
Hawk drops

Endorphinized
woodchuck   feeling
lighter than he's ever
felt before
does not think

Well that's the end

does not think

Tis better to be
wild and furry once
than never to be
wild at all

does not think

Evil hawk cruel death

does not think

What a view what a life
this is it wow
this is how it should be
forever

does not think

into the rarefied
pure air
of

does not think

flying

forever

GUELPH, SUMMER 1983

SOMETHING I'VE BEEN MEANING TO TELL YOU
for Kathy on her 35th birthday

When on that day the clouds
hugged the earth
and that fool truck decided
to run a green light

you found yourself suddenly
hovering
in pure peaceful lightness
above a strange car wreck

and the little white salamander
that slippery translucent nymph
with the feathery gills
whom I cannot quite bring
to light, who lives just beyond
the farthest thing from my mind

gave out a quick
amphibious cry, just once
enough to pierce the mortal dark

and I could feel it
like a heart, tremble in my hands
wet with blood, or with fear

When on that day
in soft wings' flutter you
from death's lightness returned
lay stiffly on the metal cart
squeezed my hand

the slim blind newt
slipped away
to just beyond my tongue's tip
blessed   blessed

into the silence

GUELPH, SEPTEMBER 1984

ALL HANDS ON DECK
for Rose and Dan, at their wedding

Blessed be the hands that bind
the apron strings behind
Blessed be the tongue that ties itself
Blessed be the loving mind
Blessed be the heart that beats for thee
Blessed be the feet that beat the clock
to get here   just in time

But most of all blessed be the hands
that all join hands
that give a hand
to whip the cream
the hands that shake
the hands   thumbs up
whose thumbs are green

Blessed be the hand
that has the bird in
blessed the hand that feeds thee
blessed the hand that rocks the cradle
blessed the hands
the whole world's in

Blessed be the handy ends of arms
Blessed be the end of the arms race
Blessed be the policy of hands off
Blessed be the laying on of hands
Blessed be the old hands
the young hands   hand in hand

What you were is out of your hands
What you are is handsome
What you will become
cannot be guessed beforehand

Blessed be on every hand this troth
It is your handle in the hurricane: do not let go

GUELPH, SEPTEMBER 1981

WHAT TO PRAY FOR

Rebecca   lying in bed
stares blue-eyed into the space
just below the stippled ceiling
where God must surely be
kicks up her pink pyjama-clad legs
and prays   Please God let no one
in the whole world
be sick or lonely

That's impossible   says Matthew
when she's done   She balks
at his realism   rolls over
and goes to sleep in protest

The next night legs tucked modestly
under the covers   she prays   Please God
let no one in the whole world get sick
most of the time
and let Oma and John Rempel
not be lonely

GUELPH, FALL 1984

GENERATIONS
for Andreas

Matthew tells me
that every day another species
disappears
When mother sea turtles clamber up the beach
people cut pieces
right out of the shell
for jewellery
Baleen whales are killed
for no apparent reason

Tonight at bedtime he says   Dad
You know how Nature
is always changing?
Well I want something different
for next Christmas
a real Transformer
What you bought me this year
was a Decepticon

(They looked the same to me)
Decepticons are the bad guys
he says   Transformers are good
At seven years he tells me parables
sees through my accretion of masks
my masquerades of change

Of course I am imagining this precocity
yet where else do our children dwell
but in the heavens/hells we think for them?
This is the essence is it not of *minding* children?
I feel myself coming loose
like Matthew's tooth bleeding at the gums
where Melissa bumped him at recess
Another parental sacrifice
to the cosmic tooth fairy

For a brief strange period
his tongue will speak into the gap
and then a new sharp tooth will push up
into a world I cannot imagine

GUELPH, JANUARY 1985

ENDANGERED SPECIES
for Dave, Mary, Emilie, Lauren and Lindi
a farewell poem

I. THE DISAPPEARANCE

When your friends leave
you are a shrub

and they are a snake
whose head thinks itself
already across the path
but whose body remains
entangled in you

They are a cat who clings
pulled away from you
so you are torn
by the persistence of its love

They are crows
who leave in the Fall   not knowing
they will return

II. THE SIGHTING

I sit in a boat
on an unruffled lake
mist paling in the muffled dawn
The water breaks   sploosh
just at the edge of my vision

I look to see a spray
of silver flowers trailing
silver rippling necklace rings
encircling
an empty centre

I am not sure
what I have seen
I can only report
I am not sure
what I am remembering
what might have been

Two loons drift by
into the lifting mist
three little ones
paddling madly after

GUELPH, SEPTEMBER 1984

SILENCE: IT IS NEVER THE SAME

Silence just before
the jackhammer hammering
and the stunned second
after   peace
before the bullet's snap
and in the deer's soft
answer   warm repose
before the robin's spring aubade
and when the geese have fled
dumb cold

the long silence of a friend
reading in the same room
and the long silence of a friend
half a world gone

GUELPH, WINTER 1984-85

THE MIND
A nightly life cycle based on *Dictyostelium disocidium,* a slime
mould, which is sometimes a plant, and sometimes an animal
for Bill and Pat

In the wake of sun's departure
the mind stirs   pulls up its roots
and scatters   The skull cannot hold
these amoeba   They slink
to the corners of the backworld
to the compost heaps and yogurt tubs
of Everyday gone decadent

The mind feeds on these things
things of reverberating substance
the reverberations of substance
matter transubstantiated into God
knows what   hyena's death-laugh   the crows'
scavenging craw   the impudent lifeburst of pollywogs
the momentary permanence of marigolds

This is not death
This is a preparation   See
my grandfather is here   He will tell you
about teaching in the Ukraine   He knows
about the Revolution   He can explain
death   that perfection
of the mind's animal   a prowling
between stars   flicking
of tongues   fins and legs
in matter's resonance
innocence in love perfected

Death is not returning
from this nightplace   not morning when
the mindslugs cringe unto themselves
become a sorocarp on spine's stalk
nerve rootlets and a puff of dreamspores
and in the brittle sunrise
my self

SASKATOON, AUGUST 1978

THE HEART'S DANCE

The heart like a performing bear
wearies of the tricks
the tongue's chain
her garland of metal rings
the pain   wearies of this
dance   this public teaser
played before
a crowd of twinkling eyeballs

The bear thinks
rocks crags trees
thinks lumbering down between
hills   snort of muscled fur
the flinging bite of fish flesh
in deep cave pools

In this dance   the tongue calls
all the cues   the eyeballs roll
throw money   It's a living
this dance   this regulated motion
this

bear remembers   tears
his chain   his snout
from tongue asunder
fleeing
between the hills
where falling thunder mystifies
the air   in the sightless
dark   in the salt of his blood
speechless

dancing for no one
the lup-dub
the comely
slow   lonely
dance of the heart

GUELPH, AUGUST 1984

POEM FOR MY FRIENDS
(a poem to tell directions in the woods)

I wish you days with their skin
split open, like a mangosteen staining your hands
like wine, like memories
turning in sweet segments
like cool white fish
over and over
on your tongue
in your mind

I wish you nights
cupped like an empty wineglass
turning in your hand, and you are barefoot
in a dark wood; leaves brush your face
and smooth, stone-like fruits
are at your feet.
You are recalling your fine day
and where you rest your palm
against the bark
I shall be for you
a soft and friendly moss

GUELPH, MAY 1987

31

NEW DIRECTIONS IN GROWING
for Dave, at 35

The tree in the swamp
starts with big claws for feet
then sneaks up
up greenily tasting
the fresh blue sky and stretching out
a branchy yawn

At thirty-five
the feet give out
and the tree changes directions.
Waving his roots
like angelfins in the air
he cuts away
a flash of silver
in the swamp of life

GUELPH, JULY 1987

THE BIG ONE
for Allan Secord

When you go after the big one
pray he doesn't bite too soon
Take joy in sun on water
a cool breeze just at dawn
Take time to tie the flies
just right   to listen for the song
of loons   A whole day just to breathe the air
is not too long
Trade stories with a friend
Share the small fries   sizzling on a fire
Take note of changes in the wind
the whisper of leaves
so when dusk murmurs its secrets
through the trees
and out over the stream
when the big one breaks in silver splendour
the peace behind you   you will know
the final catch brings no regrets
only a waking from the beauty
of this dream

GUELPH, MARCH 1983

II
THAT OLD SCRAP AGAIN

THERE MIGHT NOT BE A NUCLEAR WAR

A frog is an unexpected
state of mind
I am standing up to my meninges
in cold breakers   checking over
fossilized cephalopods   My grey matter
is full of them   Lifting up
a large slab of dura
mater   I spot him
a green leopard frog

Startled   he blinks   thinks
I may not see him   leaps
as I reach for him   squirms
into a watery sulcus
I laugh at having thought
such a silly thing
I hope he will be there
again tomorrow

BIG BAY, ONTARIO, AUGUST 1983

THAT OLD SCRAP AGAIN

After hearing Pat Lane advocate heart over mind at the
Blue Mountain Poets' Festival in the summer of 1980

The heart pleads   she begs
she hammers at the door
Old noggin   coconut dictator
will not let her out
Her arterial hand
like a prehensile tail
snakes out between the bars
drags herself   all rage and bloody
tears   on to his sleeve
He grabs her by the logic
That old scrap again

How they go at it
the heave of love and the thrust
of death commingled
the body exploding to a thousand bits
in the dust   gone to seed
The crows scatter in a cloud
The cloud contracts to feed

I need them both   the heart's witch
and the brain's petty tyrant
There's a Nazi in the bowels
of my good germanic soul
He will blow off the brain
He will strangle the heart
He will kill one of them
to better rule the other
Old heartless nut   headless pump
let us become a Canada
impossibly joined
by the crotch of our ventricles
It is our only defence
against the murderous discipline

GUELPH, FALL 1980

39

CONVERSION EXPERIENCE
to Conrad, for a wonderful sermon on war toys

The Powers were everywhere
the still small voice   stilled
Leaves I heard   or fresh cold snow
or steam   perhaps   escaping
My heart was tamed   my brain professioned
the untrustworthy rhythms of my blood   re-schooled
the black tunnels of my id   mined
I was being packaged for export
I was being run in the national interest
I was only following orders

Sneaking down the back alleys of my gut
ready for my soul's ignominious exit
in a cloud of gas   there in the foulest dungeon
I almost tripped over Him
My God what are you doing here!
Coward! He answered *Fool! Traitor! Get back
there!*

Stung   as in a prairie blizzard
I reeled back through whimpering
bloodswamps   up   clambering
the cold rocks of power
into the trees no forest
can be seen for
The government was caught off guard
by the pure rage of my love
Was this a brief? a speech?
Had I come before the wrong committee?
They wanted my credentials
Was I a royal commission? They couldn't
find the right papers   They wanted
to be out of opposition   They wanted
to be in luck   They wanted

to deal with the issues   They wanted
to see my social insurance number

I do not remember it all
my tongue a whip   the tables overturned
Not alone I was   we were
in the streets again   doctors
cooks diaper washers computer scientists
poets farmers God help us even veterinarians
all of us singing arresting traffic
without a warrant   unscrewing
the missiles at our backs   unhinging
the industry of death
singing around a great fire
enough to make even the most tempered
of steel hearts soften   singing
with our children in our arms   wondering
at our lack of professional decor   wondering
at the money we were losing   not being
at work   wondering at the beauty
of it all

Later   I was
a child alone
in the wrecked   aged chambers of my heart
papers swirling in the wind
the hiss somewhere of steam escaping
the voice of God   perhaps
And outside
or somewhere in a guarded classroom
in my brain   the Powers re-grouping
voices of children playing Star Wars

GUELPH, NOVEMBER 1983

41

IMAGES OF PEACE
a poem in six parts

I. PRECONDITIONS FOR NEGOTIATION

The basis for negotiation is slaughter
Animists have slaughtered atheists have
slaughtered Christians have
slaughtered Muslims have
slaughtered B'hais Catholics have
slaughtered Lutherans Calvinists have
slaughtered Mennonites Communists have
slaughtered Capitalists have Jews Arabs have
slaughtered   In person by proxy you have
slaughtered   Yes deep in your heart
if it was not Stalin not Hitler at the very least
you could have throttled the neighbour
whose dog crapped on your lawn

Pacify eliminate put to sleep do away with keep the peace
police capitally punish normalize protect save carry out justice
these are the words we use to justify
to eulogize our slaughter
They are the strategies of hate
the lies from which
we make ourselves

The only true basis for negotiation
is not righteousness is not strength
is nothing but the slaughter we so euphemize

On our knees let us join
our bloody minds

II. THE UKRAINE, 1922

Father in the stone-floored kitchen
crying
I heard
My ear against the hardness
Eight years old
Lord
Wish I were deaf
Do you hear?

Father in the kitchen
crying Mother Mother
all the men   teacher Willms' brother
the carpenter   all
over in Neu Halbstadt
gathered in the school cellar
packed in
Teach you something
they snorted

Butchers they
bashed in blades slashing
heads and bellies
Pigs

Barred doors
no visitors till morning
All night   their moans
hung in the stifled room
into the stone-cold dawn
a cellar full of meat
bellies ears heads arms
black as bloodwurst

Crying
I heard
Father
Stone-cold
deaf   Wish I were
Like the stones   even
crying

Father

III. THE LEBANON, 1982

Mother Father Child
lined up
against the wall   family portrait
Here is the flash
Look at the birdie   a skewered dove
Say cheese   Here is the negative
fixed in blood
A moment to remember

Who ordered these pictures
my fellow Christians?
Who took them too far
away?   I do not recognize
Yosef Miriam Y'shua   Jews you say?
Christians? Blow them up
Look again   Palestinians? People? They are
blurred   Still   I do not know
them   Blow them up   Look
the photographer on his knees blowing
himself up   I do not know him
Who gave the orders? Blow him
up   there   if you look
between the people   it is a wall
only a wall   Ha ha   no family
was taken   Such a relief   a wall
a base relief

This inquiry is over
Blessed be the name of relief

IV. GUATEMALA, 1983

Adelaida Aleman
pretty roundbellied sister
Mother of Hope
when they gathered the village
together in the church   your family
before you
before they
was there a voice
in the flames   a whisper
among the screams?
Did the guardia kneel?
soul's eyes stung
by the incensed smoke?

Adelaida Aleman
Mother of Jesus
when the guardia's slitting steel
tongue licked your neck
split your belly
sick angry young man possessing
death   death's clammy flesh
when he took the boy
seven months Wholly Child seven months
held the boy   *This is my flesh*
Do this in remembrance
when he threw it to the dogs

was there the upward beat of wings?
a scream in the wind?

This poem is based on a report which appeared in The Amnesty International Bulletin *in the summer of 1983.*

V. FOR EVER AND EVER
after a poem by Rabindranath Tagore

On the seashore of the ending
world   world without end
the children play
On the endless sand
by the deafening surf
they play with hand grenades
old bombs   half buried
unsprung land mines
By the endless foaming
mouth of the sea   the deathening pound
they play catch with hand grenades
ride the old bombs   tugging
at rusty switches

The sea surges up with laughter
while their pudgy fingers
gather old land mines   gas bottles   matches
while the world is paralyzed
with terrified soap opera fear
The children laugh and dance
the dance of undertows and rusty gatling guns
They play at being jellyfish
They play man-o-war
the world's heart stung
stunned beyond weeping
in pain   clenched

From a report on Darlene Keju-Johnson's description, to the World Council of Churches, of the aftermath of the French and American nuclear tests in the Marshall Islands: "Most ghastly was Johnson's description of babies who are born as jellyfish. The baby is born on the labour table and it breathes and moves up and down but it is not shaped like a human being. It looks like a bag of jelly."

VI. THE NAME OF PEACE

On our knees we cry
Lord   do you hear
the beat of wings against our pain
against death's mask of sweet relief

This is no way to end a song a life
a planet
with peace but toppled images
in ruined temples
spaces in a broken poetry

Where is the Word
when all is said and done
to call the children home

John A. Toews
in World War Two worked as a chaplain
to a group of brave and dangerous
objectors   nonkillers
held in cloud-enshrouded cabins
on Canada's West Coast
—held under ban to keep them from
the public   who might believe them
or   not believing   kill them
One night   a clear   for once
and starry night   his window open
to the cool primeval pine
wombed deep in sleep
John A. was cracked awake as from a shell
by panic-stabbing feet upon his bed
A lantern   Quick   he called   A light

And there   a fawn   deer child
passingly blind   terrified
In quiet breaths   the Name worth dying for
for which we cannot kill   I AM
In wildered eyes the image   PEACE
then suddenly sprung home   gone   and yet
as in a dream
still ringing in his blood

Hear then the chaplain's song
within us   singing
against all images of slaughter
the Word singing in our bones
like a knife turning
like a Mother's gentle hand

The image of our pain   war's prey
lies crouched upon the silent tongue

GUELPH, NOVEMBER 1983

49

PEACEFUL LINGUISTICS

Peace is a word to be coupled with
time   at the end
at the end of a busy
a busy and repetitive workday
I long for a little
a little time for
a little
and quiet
peace   a word to be couched
with nick   as in the saint
as in a person whose conscience was nicked
in the shave of
time   a small word to be put with
out   a breather a moment to think
before the final play
for peace   a game to be wrestled
with talks which start are called off and
swing on with the mood of a popular tic
which returns us to time and to
peace   a word to be married with full
and the fulness
of time
which is our end

GUELPH, NOVEMBER 1983

ALMS FOR THE RICH

Death came begging at my door
Alms for death! Alms for death!
I gave him nothing, and something more—
I couldn't stand his fetid breath.

I need you, he cried, to defend this land,
for freedom, for peace, for all that's grand.
If you do one small job for me
I promise you immortality.

Say something bitter about a Russian,
an Arab, a Sikh, or a French-speaking Jew.
Or better yet, buy me a sub
to chase away those peacetime blues.

Oh death was fat, and rich, and clean.
He drove a Mercedes. He owned a plane.
Was clever with numbers. Explained how war
could make us rich and distract the poor.

But when death came begging at my door
His fetid tongue crying   Alms for death!
I gave him nothing, and something more—
I shall not, till my dying breath.

GUELPH, OCTOBER 1987

FOR A COLUMBIAN MOTHER

The future is a children's dance, with drums,
a violin, guitars, and a drunk man humming.

In this dance there are no men in uniform,
no guns at the bar, no guns at the street corner.

The future sings like a flute, or a rose, startling, alone
—tomorrow—gone.

Its petals fall into today, and then yesterday,
like a bottle of Aguardiente, vaguely remembered.

For a child, not remembering, all things
are possible—a snowman, a tree house, singing

a melody with no purpose
other than the pleasant following of notes.

The future will kiss your hand. He will dance
with you. He will know all the right steps.

He will rise, like a fern from soil unfurling,
like the sun, like your son, his hair

dishevelled from sleep, into a white room
with a white table, and a moist red plum.

He will smile, vaguely,
like an old man remembering a child.

BOGOTA, SEPTEMBER 23, 1987

III
SURVIVORS

THE GIFT
for Mother, who has survived revolution, civil war, drought, famine, being
orphaned, emigration, servant work, motherhood, widowhood, and much
more besides, on her 75th birthday

After the first sharp cry
it is not a question   this life
of what has been survived
It is what has survived

It is not your father gone
swarthy faces at the window   with guns
In the kitchen   it is Mother's hum
a cup of fresh warm milk   and a bun

It is not Mother reduced to the bone's
terrible whisper   nor a house abandoned
It is the train like a bright snake amid the ruins
a bird soaring   crying   in its flight home

It is not the hopelessness of loss
rude officials at greasy shipyards   and dust
It is a young woman from overseas   the kindness in her face
setting out the doctor's tea in blue china cups

Of that new land as flat as *Plautdietsch*
where even *Zwieback* loomed significant
and *Pluma Moos* for all the *Englisch* knew
was some kind of deer to shoot

and a horse a husband five bushy-haired
kids a house   several houses   one finally with no steep stairs
a real freezer for meat buns and cookies and a recreation room
to hide the television   we can really only claim

the cookies   which we did   still frozen
as our first tangible recollection
But even this   our remembering and remembering of
    remembrance
will pass   and our children's

It is not the quartz-sharp grit deeply clasped
by the heart which we inherit   nor the pain's lingering grasp
It is you   here   now   the rich opaquely buffed layers
of your life   like a pearl   before us

JAVA, JUNE 1986

56

MIND OUT OF SEASON

Windfulls of rice-like snow
lash against autumn's brown
wrinkled face

The birds leave

Fat squirrels sleep
in hollow trees
Snow like shreds of wedding lace
wisps around the branches

Unexpectedly in midwinter
it rains
All is mudbrown and hesitant
greens   one confused squirrel
climbs out among the silent limbs
She is held there   as if in the arms
of a bent and disillusioned saint

Like a widow she ponders
the rudeness of this awakening
I throw her some peanuts
She disappears
thinking this is an attack
I think about the death of fathers
and the migration of birds

The crows are too far south
to return for this brief
this false season
smug and black-robed they await
the choir of robins humming
to the pluck of worms

I am watching for the black wing
listening for the song
As my father before me
I shall sing my equivocal chorus
robed in the soiled tatters
of this broken earth

BARRIE, JANUARY 1980

A KIND OF RESURRECTION
*for B.C. 'Bun' Patterson, who survived a heart attack; every kid should be
so lucky, to have a father like that.*

A man could be almost happy
were his golf swing a little cleaner
were not the road so tense with ice
were the grandchildren not quite so noisy
as they fart their cars across the carpet

were there not this sharp snagging snakebite
at the heart, this writhing
in the ribcage, this plunge
down the black lightning
to a shocked ground.

Floating back up through layers of fluid light
a man thinks about the simple, firm joy
of his club's swing up, sunward
(who cares where the ball goes?),
the dazzling shadows of his footprints in the snow
(see I'm not gone yet),
and the sheer power he can impart to his granddaughter's car
by putting his tongue between his lips
and singing thbthbthbthb.

Sitting there on the carpet
in a pool of sunlight
drenched in a shower of kids' giggling
a man can, yes, really,
a man can be happy.

GUELPH, EASTER 1987

TAKING HEART
for Winnie, after a recovery from a heart attack

After a day of giving speeches
your voice goes
After a life of giving a listening ear
your heart
suddenly, on stage, says
enough
and you are floating away
voiceless, all peaceful heart
with no body to burden it down.
When you wake up
you are sitting in a chair
sunlight flying down through the window.
It lands in your lap
plop!
full of furry surprise
and little sharp claws
like a golden cat
with feathers on his whiskers

purring

GUELPH, EASTER 1987

THE DAY BEFORE WINTER IN SUTHERLAND

November lawns in Sutherland
are unshorn bristly and frost-white
like the chin of an old man

He is shuffling along 110th Street
in a heavy sweater denim jacket and jeans
and a new railroad engineer's cap

The bare-jointed trees moan
arthritically with cold

Just now Old Man
is going up to get groceries
from the corner   so he said to Old Woman
knitting by the cat   Soon it will snow
she said   rubbing her hands together

Old Man is not so sure
It has been a good Fall   Up the street
he hears the squeal of steel on steel
spine-tingling music of train wheels
fierce roar of diesel at the crossing

Old Man has sap running
in his limbs   vigour in the thump
of his cane   At Central Avenue
the thunder of boxcar greeting boxcar
claps him on the back like an old friend

Sparks spray across the nightsky in his skull
Transfixed by celebration he stands
leaning on his cane   steam breath
hissing out in short spurts

The iron boxcar hands clasp
as CPR one-oh-seven-four is rescued
emptybellied and cold as an orphanchild
from the siding   Gently
he is eased into the fellowship of rails

Flashing lights and bells applaud at the crossing
Car drivers honk impatient for this tedious
ritual to end   By the time
the last red-faced car has clicked past
the engine is puffing out across the prairie openness
bounding along stiff rails like a puppy
with children laughing after

One car is left behind on the siding
Some men are prying at the door
The car creaks and groans in all its joints

Old Man   after the long block home
sets a bag of groceries down
on the kitchen table   Tomorrow for sure
he says
it will snow

SASKATOON, FALL 1978

62

TANTE TINA'S CHRISTMAS, 1983
  (or The Real Mennonite Way)

Me it's not
what they want
It's my stories

Tell us how it was
they ask me, imagine
my boy Hänschen and his little Hänschen
not so long ago just a little *Knirps*
but now already with an *Anhängsel*. These girls
don't like me to say it so,
like they are something hanging on, but with names like
Angela and Mary-Jean what else can I think?
Such names aren't Mennonite, that's sure.
But I love them, ja, they're my Hänschens'.
What can I tell?
So is das Leben.

Christmas afternoon the boys still groan
from too much turkey and potatoes,
eat *Halvah* and play *Knipsbrat*
and the kids go out down the riverbank
tobogganning.
It's the same, like it was.
And before that, even,
Weinachtsabend, after the children's program
at church—you know little Hänschen
read a Scripture this year?
Even with his hair so long
they let him read, praise God—even then,
before the plates for each child
under the tree go, we all sing
"Welch ein Jubel, Welche Freude,"
so nothing new under the sun comes.
I get older only.

Now they want stories,
how I walked to school in snow,
they want *Russlända* stories
from Opa and Oma.
Once, I tell them, we didn't all think
we could save the world.
That the Lord's work was.
Now even the girls go to college,
and what can they do?
A world without *Porzeltche*
is not worth saving, or *Zwieback* at least,
or *Borscht* and *Rollkuchen*,
but what do they know of that?

Anyhow one time the *Machnovites* came
to our house in the Molotschna.
Everyone they would kill, they said, but Mutti
had *Borscht* in a big *Topf*   steaming
and the men when they must choose
between their guns and a spoon for the *Borscht*
every time the spoon wins.
The soldiers ate themselves *sat*
and went away, so you see? The Lord provides.
Hänschen he likes that story
but his *Frau* the *Anhängsel* is not so sure.

Then I tell them
Well, that was my *Weinachtswünsch*,
where is yours, and Hänschen, you know,
living in that big house with an *englische Frau*
he can still say

"Da war einmal ein Mann
Er hatte eine Pfann
Die Pfann war ihm zu heiss
So ging er auf das Eis, u.s.w."
so I am happy.
And little Hänschen the grandboy with the hair
he can sing with the guitar
"Hänschen klein ging allein
in die Weite Welt hinein . . ."

All around we sit in the *Grautestov*
with my Hänschen in his fancy shoes
and his Hänschen in bluejeans
and the girls not even one of us
who would say we *mennonitisch* are?

How we think, even,
is all *aufgemixed.*
Big Hänschen has his head all full of Social Credit
and little Hänschen preaches the N.D.P.,
but you can still see it,
it's the same, how they walk
the real Mennonite way,
like bringing in the cows.

ELKHART, INDIANA, CHRISTMAS 1983

65

TANTE TINA REFLECTS ON MAGGIE THATCHER
for Jim Reimer

That woman, *ach du Lieber,*
no sauce on her *Verenicke*
she's got, that's what, too much
pasty dough and two percent milk.
She should come to *Sengerfest*
and sing along with the other old ladies.
O that I had a thousand tongues
she should like,
not all this stuff of never giving in.
She gave in long ago.
To rest by Ronald Reagan on his horse
her mind was laid.
Kids, even, they have,
runt weanlings with diaper pins
in their ears, a hopeless bunch,
rock throwers, pinches off the old dough ball herself,
left too long in the oven,
like *geröstete Zwieback.*

Maggie herself,
she too is *geröstet.*
She needs dipping in some tea,
get those buns wet,
a good immersion baptism, and then
Confession: *Lieben sie die Brueder?*
Let her confess before the whole church
how she found the Lord
right here at Tina's place.
Let her confess how she came down
one night, and Tina plied her with *Paska*
and *Glums,* Tina ladled all that *Pluma Moos*
out of her head,
gave her potatoes to think about,
where they come from, and eggs,

let her shovel some of that other stuff
the chickens make,
she makes so well herself,
gave her *Halvah* just to keep the plumbing clear.

Let her confess how Tina made *Verenicke*
and Jim Reimer himself made the sauce
so good the Lord would eat.
Ach, Mrs. Thatcher, come down to Altona.
Change your name: Magdalena Thiessen
is much nicer, ja?
Flop your buns down in the kitchen here.
Confess a little. It's good for the bunyans.
So bad the world can't be
there's no hope.
You just come down here to Tina's,
we'll get you back in shape.
Then we can do something
about those men.

GUELPH, LATE 1983

TANTE TINA CALLS IN TO A RADIO TALK SHOW

Hello? Is this the radio?
The talk-in show? Ja, it's me
Tina again. Like a pig this thing squeals.
Turn my radio down? Just a minute. O.K.

Ja, now I think the Russian
invasion of Grenada—pardon?
ja, I mean the American invasion
of Afghanistan—no, ja,
you know what I mean,
like the British when they came to Manitoba
when Louis Riel was here.
That's when the Harry Dick family
from our village in Russia came
but they went to Mexico, because here it was all
so *englisch*, you know?
But now his children
are coming back. Better *Knacksaut* here
I say, ha ha. Ja, Altona is the sunflower
capital of Canada. Harry Dick
he was my mother's uncle.
Tante Kate, she stayed here.
Twelve children, she told Uncle Fritz,
I'm not going to Fernheim
just for no rubber tires.
But some, like the Peter Dicks,
they went too and liked it.
No, I don't think they went to Grenada.
But Harry Peters, when he left Russia,
he came through Afghanistan,
and his children are now missionaries in India.

Ja, O.K., I'll be short.
What my idea is,
I think they should all come back
to Manitoba—pardon?
Ja, I don't care, the Russians, Americans, the Harry Dicks,
whoever. My Tante Frieda, she's still in Russia,
at Alma Ata, and Lydia Franz's boy Fred,
he lives in America, in Fresno.
So you see?

O.K., I have to go now.
The *Platz* is burning.

GUELPH, LATE 1983

WINNIPEG
for Hildi, a fellow refugee

"Then if any man say unto you, Lo, here is Christ, or there; believe
it not." Matthew 24:23

That night we had wave
after crashing wave of thunder
bouldering down the clouds
I could almost imagine Winnipeg again
God come down in Edmonton or Toronto
or some other God-forsaken place
and Winnipeg   she there on her knees
rinsing her soiled hair
in the Red   the Assiniboine snaking
at her skirts   she so cursing angry
shrieking *Plautdietsch* at Portage and Main
    To have come so far
    half-way around the world
    and still to have missed the Chosen Place
    it must not be!

    The real Messiah will come singing
    Handel to Winnipeg   reeking of *Borscht*
    and *Rollkuchen   Porzeltche* and *Paska*
    round as a laughing buddha
    but not laughing   serious   like raw cabbage
    or an uprooted potato   but not so offensively poor
    a washed potato perhaps   singing
    certainly   a baritone   a fine baritone
    good enough for Hymn Sing
    and after him a whole cherubic chorus
    singing *Kernlieder*
    singing the Halleluja Chorus
    singing   for a grand finale
    just before the food
    Praise God from Whom All Blessings Flow

And here in this smug country
in the middle of a summer storm
I could almost imagine the Aryan devil
come down in Winnipeg   singing Wagner
the clashes here but faint reverberations
of that mad embrace
the ecstasy of fierce frustration
        See God what you have missed!
the live-hate scream thundering
from see to churchly see

And I could almost imagine us
sitting with Jesus   a lean and barely laughing
loin-clothed raconteur   in Edmonton or Toronto
drinking wine from fingerbowls
from the washroom tap   feeling just a little
sentimental   drawing circles
with our fingers on the table
waiting
for another parable
waiting
for the storm to pass over
looking up to see Him gone   suddenly
and in the distance   from Winnipeg perhaps
the exquisite consummation
Bach's Magnificat
in Low German

GUELPH, JULY 1981

71

ICELAND
to Asta, Jon-bjorn, Jona and Yngvi

Discontented   full of violent
devotions   I sipped cold comfort
from night's chalice   heard
no music   nor the fierce missile sent

burning from the gods' frontier
too late felt the watery plunge
the rock crust broken   the strange
and joyful pain of man's career

And here where lava bled
and red rock lips broke
silence   in tongues of smoke
I knew another life and faced my death

In time   congealing   time counted
but in centuries   young greens
graced rocks   then ships were seen
then flags   buildings   people mounted

Men and women counted each
other   children triumphed over rocks
put down roots   hung out socks
to dry   set fish out on the beach

In sod huts   in snow   by fire
they recreated selves in stories   poetry
and in that act created earth and sea
and in the long night   the sun's faint choir

And now   at peace   hold civilized opinions
warm houses with hot lava   In one domain
share coffee   rum   sweet belly-filling cakes
and argument   and no one holds dominion

GUELPH, NOVEMBER 1983

BIRDS
for Matthew and Rebecca, in an election year

The ring-bills cruise this rocky shoreline
Jonathan Livingston teenagers
out looking for a quick nirvana
the flick of fishtails
through the shattered bluegreen glass
of the lake
They've got the white noise
up full breaker   blasting rocky stuff
new wave   the folksy waxwings' evensong
jammed off the air

At least they're flying   At Sauble Beach
the little kid from Hamilton screams Italian
at them   throws them popcorn
and fast food leftovers   They hop and mock-
squeal ecstasy   argh argh
The kid loves it
They play him up for all the bee-bop
he's worth   but already their beady little eyes
are on my picnic lunch
Hey   I'm a Mennonite I got a legal exemption
lay off

In Saskatoon they cycle
and recycle over garbage bins
and white-brimmed sloughs
In Georgia Strait these Icaroids hang
down by docks and ships' butt ends

Is this it then?
Our dream keepers   political elites
of every feather   have come
to this?   Popcorn catchers
and beach peckers?
Is this the human flight dream
like a pock-marked moon
come home to roost?
Where is that laughing grace
the flight of eyebrows
etched against a rising sun?

We are a people of fattened dreams
look carefully   how we have fed them
In Guelph the geese in autumn gather
practise flight formations low and startling
over rooftops north south east west
returning always to the park
where they are fed   All winter
north south east west geese leaving
geese returning   *In Winnipeg*
I counsel Matthew and Rebecca
the geese once left   left once
returned a white and gooseless season later
They nod   But how can I explain
the substance of this sign
the constancy   the voice of God
the Spirit in the form of

74

My children   listen
a myriad of birds swirling diving
darting skimming the sky all
bellyfull of feathers   let this be the dream
Now   say the dream is mortalized
plummets here in all its forms
hawks swallows gulls chickens the whole lot
And say I do an autopsy   yes
cut them open   just to see
every little dreamform dead   to understand them
Do you know what I would find?
A bird is pretty much just bird   once dead
owls and sparrows   turkeys
a nation's dreams

My children   listen
A bird in the bush
is worth two in the hand
A dream once claimed as true
is one dream gone   done
Mark the grave   Like Jacob
dream upon that stone

Dream nights full of feathered wings
geese larks ringtails fearful things

Follow them north south   within
Keep them tangible   but thin

Keep them safe from Sauble Beach
Tease them barely out of reach

And when the night is charred and bare
the dreams shall come nest in your hair

And when there is no sun nor moon
your dreams shall guide you
dreamwings bear you
skimming wavebreaks beaches rocks
garbage bins   creaking docks
soaring on the world's Wind's light
into the dream that sets all others
into joyous
panic-stricken
flight

BRUCE PENINSULA, AUGUST 1984

GIORGIO, WHERE ARE YOU NOW?
a poem from Java for Pier Giorgio Di Cicco

This is the street you walk along
after a rain, the concrete glistening
under the greenish glare of streetlights.
The lights are going out.
People are settling down.

The world is blowing up.

The flies this year are irrepressible.
They buzz in my coffee cup
copulate on the rice
rest on my earlobe.
They are planning what colour the drapes will be
after the war.

This is the street from 1967 to wherever.
It is a kind of runway.
The fumes flower in my nose.
The birds are screaming in my ear.
These are not the British birds of 1967.
These are Islamic neoconservative feminists,
their habits flapping in the wind
AIDS and herpes flap flap.
I live between fear, inadequacy and,
what the hell,
eternal hope.

I am almost 40,
when life begins at.
Last birthday, a friend gave me a blowup
of a coloscopy picture, and I realized
that there is a light at the end of the tunnel
but we are at the wrong end
looking into the darkness.

The light is behind us.

This street I am on, Giorgio,
I have started running down.
I have clearance from the tower.
I am almost out of breath.
My feet rotate like wheels, like feet in a cartoon.
We can fly, Giorgio: it's all in arms control.

Arms away!

I'm lifting off.
My eyes are on the moon.
Giorgio, flying deeper into the twentieth century,
are you there?

JAVA, FEBRUARY 1987

39 LINES FOR MY 39th BIRTHDAY

When I turned 39
the first 38 years
came to the party.
The little ones
just garbled at me
and pulled at my pants.
Cute, maybe
or just embarrassing,
they sat with their feet
in the sink eating cookies
telling me about old times
filling their pants.
It's the big ones
who gave me a hard time.
How's it going? asked 19.
Is there peace on earth?
Are the People Free?
And 21, cross-legged on the rug:
Build your A-frame yet?
In the woods? Eh?
And 25:
Got a Nobel Prize?
And 33 and 35 and
Have you grown up?
Have you written your Book?
Do you still get acne?
Have you learned to cook?
Can you type?
How's your tennis?
Forgotten all those things you promised?
All those years of mine
acting like friends, eating my cake,
finished my wine.
They finally fell asleep

on the floor. By midnight it was just me
and 39, talking quietly,
in particular about Nothing, and what we could do about it.
And what we should do about 40
out there in the dark, banging on the door.

GUELPH, MAY 1987

THE POET'S AMBITION
for D.C.

One life is almost
not enough to contain this
the supper dishes almost
cleared   a clutter of memories
left   like green-topped silver-bottomed fish
flashing in a quick roll
on Sarangan's green lake bed

Marylove screaming in her birth bed
you ejected   a shooting
starry-eyed almost father yes
and then father in the taxi
alone in the city's relieving night

And the time at Mount Lawu
you traced the curves of Scorpio
across the tropic sky
stung with the memory of Botswana
where you could see clear down
to the razor's edge
where the fireball desert sun
flowered suddenly from night's black sand

And when on LSD you stripped
regressing in the park to Adam
to Eden to a police cruiser
City of Ottawa

Or Emilie at three snoring a duet
with Stephane Grappelli in concert
the perfect childlikeness of newborn jazz

These broken shells I gather
prod the hermit crabs of joy and pain
from their encrusted gloom
I want to gather all the fleeting beasties
want to love my neighbour as myself
like a sausage in your skin
the poet's the lover's life ambition
to love whom you love perfectly
jealously to recreate to become
those lives I have not been   yet
your life for instance

I press into my heart
what it cannot possibly contain
and like a fireworks rocket
am flung into the nightsky
these words this poem
an exhilarating burst soft fountain
of stars trailing off in smoke

Imagination's failure to become
what it imagines

The post poetic darkness opens
like a black velvet flower
faint with the scent of singed paper
and a sentimental waft of Drambuie

    JAVA, FALL 1985

*Sarangan is the name of a small lake and resort town on the higher slopes of
Mount Lawu, a volcanic mountain in central Java.*

DIVER'S TOAST
a birthday poem, for M.C.

Cake and wine   a candle both ends burning
Another year's wisdom in a friend's embrace   returning

Like island divers poised above the year's deep green
we plunge   discover wrecks unfathomed pearls unseen

Some like tourists linger   afraid to dive
Afraid their hearts will rupture   they fossilize

And if we heed fear's shark's dark gliding form
we miss the gracious angelfish   poised   unforlorn

The deeper plunge   the more the heart thumps cheer
at surfacing   Life's riches: risks   and friends held dear

GUELPH, NOVEMBER 1983

AT THE CENTRE

See the young boy in dawn's first rays
hands raised as if in prayer
his face beatific
while the thick black eels slip
writhing between his fingers
and plop back into the pail

Like those eels
substantial   moving   real
the centre slips away from me
Like an amputated leg
I feel it still

Like the proton   once registered
and measured   it changes
flits away   It cannot be
created or destroyed   As energy
it sends me spearing to the stars
In the form of mass its formless morass
pushes me sprawling on the dark
unbroken clay where nothing matters
but itself

It is the swamp buffalo
wallowing within me   seemingly
just horns and eyes and snout
giving me a sense of wet fulness
In the heat of morning sun the slow grey-
backed body pulls me through
the unseen steel edge trailing
upturning edges of my soil
I never knew were there
so dark so rich with possible new rice
I almost laugh   the cut so deep
I am weeping all along the furrow

I capture the wind
in a bottle   but when I lift
the lid   I find only musty stillness
I form all the right words
in a poem   but when I speak the lines
a great silence rings in my ears

It is making love in the afternoon
with the children in the next room
real as the bodies pressed in silent cries
ephemeral as that brief moment
alone
Like radiation   unseen
devastating in the decay it wreaks
wonderful and deadly as genetic aberrations
two-headed snakes   cyclopic fish
a body without arms
still seized with the unquenchable desire
to embrace

I cannot grasp this
I cannot let it go

I wrestle with it
as moisture struggles with the clouds
late in the Javanese day's heat-pulse
In the wrestler's clasp I fall
all in a monsoon deluge   a dizzying fall
amid the garbage the mice the frail blossoms
leaves hearts memories swept away in the flood
Flood gone   a flower sprouts
in the wet red silt
sun breaking just before it sets

Before the gardener comes
with his pail and his knife
Before the hand's soft brush
the blade's quick cut
Before the dark path   no feet
touching as they pass
Before I am held   finally
in the Light of the Beholder

I cannot say from whence
the water's drawn
I drink only
climbing by the root of my fear
from broken bricks and wood chips
clinging by a slender green hope
and the orchid's brief song

JAVA, AUGUST 1986

WHAT THIS POETRY IS ALL ABOUT

I come to you
the stem clenched in my teeth
thorns piercing lips tongue cheek
the petals at my lip soft perfect red
delicate as the torn flesh
of my speech

I speak of earth
of a garden uprooted
soil broken   fruitless now
as a woman's returning blood

My song bears
the sudden unexpected grip
of fitful memories
rife with the cool dark
vegetative scent of a root cellar

Through the opening hatch
fall the bright petals
of a November sun

GUELPH, WINTER 1984-85

AN OLD GREY WATER BUFFALO IN THE NOONDAY SUN

The tough grey buffalo
like a weary heart wallows.
Inside him, a calf kicks
up his fears and laughs.
On his back, a lone white
egret
probes at his dark places.
She lifts
slightly, to her toes,
in the breeze
then settles
like a sigh.
Under the puritanic blaze
of the sun
everything falls
still.

GUELPH, FALL 1987

TRANSLATIONS

ach du Lieber	an interjection like "oh my goodness"
Anhängsel	something that hangs on, like an ornament
aufgemixed	mixed up (a German-English mixed-up word)
Borscht	a kind of vegetable soup with beets or cabbage as the base
Da war einmal ein Mann, etc.	a children's rhyme: There once was a man He had a pan The pan was too hot for him So he went onto the ice . . . etc.
Englisch, englische	strictly speaking, English, but sometimes used to refer to anyone non-Mennonite (The noun is capitalized.)
Frau	wife
geröstete	toasted (in a slow oven)
Glums	cottage cheese
Grautestov	living room
Halvah	a sweetmeat of sesame flour and honey
Hänschen klein, etc.	a children's song: Little Hans went alone Into the wide world . . .
Kernlieder	a kind of traditional religious song, not quite a hymn
Knacksaut	sunflower seeds
Knipsbrat	crokinole
Knirps	kid
Lieben sie die Brueder?	Do you love the Brethren?
Machnovites	followers of Nestor Machno, a Russian anarchist who raided the Russian Mennonite colonies during the revolution and civil war
mennonitisch	Mennonite
Paska	a sweet Easter bread

Platz	a kind of crumb cake topped with fruit
Plautdietsch	Low German
Pluma Moos	a cold fruit soup
Porzeltche	raisin fritters made especially for New Year's
Rollkuchen	a kind of deep-fried pastry
Russlända	in this context, Mennonites who came from Russia
sat	satisfied
Sengerfest	a kind of hymn-sing-along at church
So is das Leben	So is life
Topf	pot
Verenicke	a kind of dumpling, filled with fruit or cheese and served with a white sauce
Weinachtsabend	Christmas Eve
Weinachtswünsch	"Christmas Wish," a poem, song or story performed as part of a family gathering on Christmas Eve or Christmas Day
Welch ein Jubel, Welche Freude	a traditional German Mennonite carol
Zwieback	two-piece buns